LINDA GRANFIELD

ALL ABOUT NIAGARA FALLS

FASCINATING FACTS, DRAMATIC DISCOVERIES

MORROW JUNIOR BOOKS · NEW YORK

For my parents,
Joseph and Barbara Granfield,
with love & thanks

The publisher gratefully acknowledges the assistance
of the Canada Council and the Ontario Arts Council
in the production of this book.

First published in Canada in 1988 by Kids Can Press
Ltd., 585½ Bloor Street West, Toronto, Ontario,
Canada M6G 1K5.

Printed in the United States of America.

1 2 3 4 5 6 7 8 9 10

LIBRARY OF CONGRESS
Library of Congress Cataloging-in-Publication Data
Granfield, Linda.
  All about Niagara Falls : fascinating facts, dramatic
discoveries / Linda Granfield.
      p.   cm.
  Includes index.
  Summary: An illustrated introduction to Niagara
Falls including a variety of historical and geographical
facts and anecdotes. Also includes a list of things to do.
  ISBN 0-688-08810-4 (pbk.)
  ISBN 0-688-08456-7 (lib. bdg.)
  1. Niagara Falls (N.Y. and Ont.)—Juvenile
literature. [1. Niagara Falls (N.Y. and Ont.)] I. Title.
F127.N8G68 1989
971.3'39—dc 19   88-13408   CIP   AC

Contents

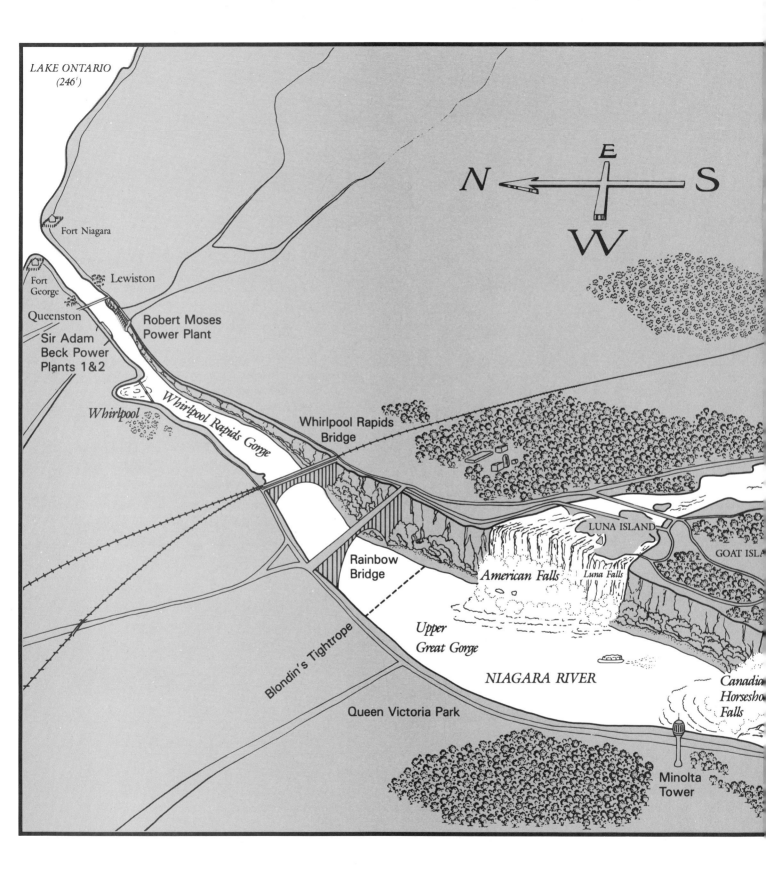

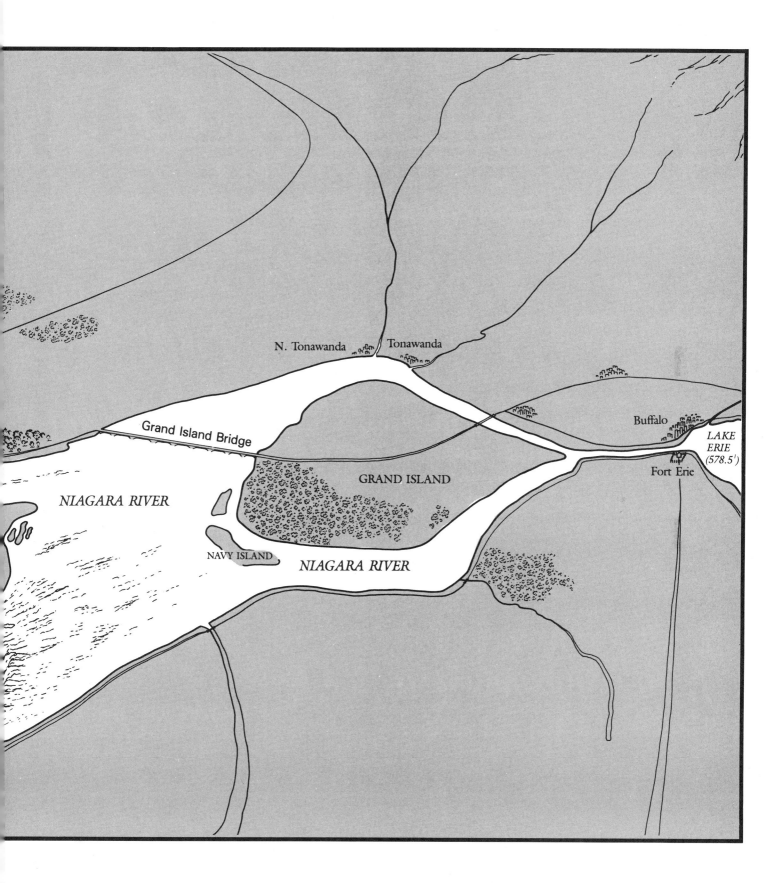

Acknowledgments

First things first: many thanks to Valerie Hussey and Ricky Englander at Kids Can Press for asking me "how about Niagara Falls?" and to Val Wyatt whose editorial skills and friendly guidance made this a most enjoyable experience.

Thanks as well to Wendy Jackson, Eileen Pilby, Glenys Biggar and Jim Whiteway of Ontario Hydro; Kenneth Macpherson, formerly of the Archives of Ontario; Harley Smith of the St. Lawrence Seaway Authority; and Dan Glenney at Fort George, Niagara-on-the-Lake, Ontario.

Gratitude is also extended to Frank Roma and Ron Kozar of the New York Power Authority; Josine Jeffery and Karen Smith of the Royal Ontario Museum, Toronto; the historical interpreters at Old Fort Niagara, New York; and George Bailey of the Niagara Parks Commission, whose boxes of photographs were like so many treasure chests.

I thank Michael Solomon for his design talents and humor, and the friends who suffered my unbridled storytelling about the Falls — and remained my friends.

Finally, I repeat my boundless gratitude to Cal, Devon, and Brian Smiley, for putting up with disrupted daily life and tours through drenching rainstorms and for providing the understanding and hugs needed to get the job done. I am indeed theirs till Niagara Falls!

"Yours Till Niagara Falls..."

No one knows where this saying comes from, but it has been written thousands of times in autograph books, school yearbooks and letters. It is a pledge of undying love and friendship.

Many people don't think of love and friendship when they think of the Falls. Instead they picture daredevils in barrels, amusement parks and game arcades. But there is more to see and learn at Niagara Falls than you might think. For example, did you know that

- bloody battles have been fought within blocks of the Falls?
- *coureurs de bois* and native people, soldiers and runaway slaves have met there at various times?
- ghosts have been seen in the area?
- power from the Falls lights millions of homes and factories?

Those hypnotic, rushing waters invite you to discover more about the mysteries and powers of Niagara Falls.

HOW IS ROBIN HOOD DIFFERENT FROM NIAGARA FALLS?

ONE HAS A LONGBOW, THE OTHER HAS A RAINBOW!

CHAPTER 1

Twenty Great Things to do at Niagara Falls

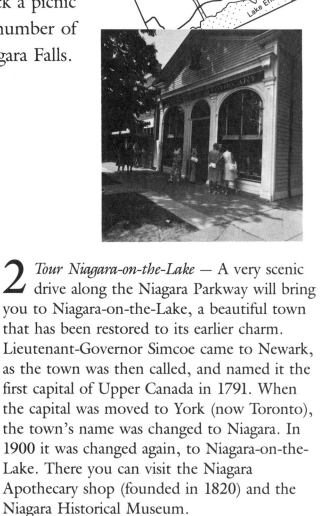

I F you're planning to become one of the millions of tourists visiting Niagara Falls, you may wonder what to do after you've gaped at the Falls. Pack a picnic lunch and stay the day. You can pick any number of these 20 "things to do" at and around Niagara Falls.

1 *Take a picture* — Everyone, including tiny children, carries a camera at Niagara Falls. If there are more than 12 million visitors each year, and even half of them take photographs, imagine how many pictures of the Falls exist in this world. There isn't an angle of the great Falls that hasn't been photographed.

2 *Tour Niagara-on-the-Lake* — A very scenic drive along the Niagara Parkway will bring you to Niagara-on-the-Lake, a beautiful town that has been restored to its earlier charm. Lieutenant-Governor Simcoe came to Newark, as the town was then called, and named it the first capital of Upper Canada in 1791. When the capital was moved to York (now Toronto), the town's name was changed to Niagara. In 1900 it was changed again, to Niagara-on-the-Lake. There you can visit the Niagara Apothecary shop (founded in 1820) and the Niagara Historical Museum.

3 *Cross a bridge* — Many bridges span the Niagara River. Among them is the Rainbow Bridge, built to replace the Honeymoon Bridge, which collapsed in an ice jam in 1938. It connects Niagara Falls, New York, with Niagara Falls, Ontario. The Peace Bridge, opened in 1927, connects Buffalo, New York, and Fort Erie, Ontario. It was named to celebrate the peace maintained along the Canada–U.S. border. The Whirlpool Rapids Bridge, built in 1897, replaced the world's first suspension bridge. From the Lewiston-Queenston Bridge you can get a fine view of the Robert Moses Power Plant and drive on into New York State, crossing over part of the plant's forebay.

The Honeymoon Bridge was destroyed by powerful ice jams in 1938.

4 *Collect licence plates* — Visitors to Niagara Falls come from every state, province and territory, as well as from other continents. When you visit the Falls, make a list of the places represented by licence plates. In just *one* parking area near Table Rock House we spotted 27 states and provinces. Can you do better?

REBECCA G. BIGGAR
FIRST WHITE CHILD BORN ON NIAGARA FRONTIER SEPT. 26, 1786 8 D'YS AFTER HER PARENTS WALKED FROM NEW JERSEY TO BENDER FARM DIED OCT. 8, 1880 HER PARENTS INTERRED IN LUNDYS LANE

5 *Visit a cemetery* — You can learn a lot from visiting a cemetery established during the days of the settlers. For example, notice how large families were then and how many children died at birth or when very young. Colonel James Fitzgibbon (see page 28) and his wife, Mary, were married in 1814 and quickly had one daughter and four sons, all healthy. Then 12 more children were born, but they all died young. How many families do you know who have had 17 children? Visit Drummond Hill cemetery on Lundy's Lane, where Laura Secord is buried.

6 *Eat a peach* — Or buy some preserves. Many of the Loyalists who settled on the Niagara Peninsula farmed the orchards you still see today. There are also about 14 million grapevines in the Niagara region from which wine and grape juice are made. The annual grape harvest lasts from early September to mid-October and includes the Niagara Grape and Wine Festival for 10 days at the end of September. Some harvesting is done by mechanical harvesters, the rest by hand. The rich soil of the area yields huge fruit harvests and led to the establishment of Canadian wineries. Some of the vineyards, orchards and wineries have guided tours you can take. You can also pick your own basketful of fruit to take home.

8 *Take a boat ride* — A trip to the Falls is not complete unless you've taken the wet and wonderful ride on a *Maid of the Mist*. The boats take you right up to the base of the Falls, where the noise is so loud that you can't hear the person next to you. You'll be given a raincoat to wear, but be prepared for a dripping face anyway.

7 *Spot a honeymooner* — The first famous Niagara Falls honeymooner was Jerome Bonaparte, brother of Napoleon. Jerome was married to Elizabeth Patterson of Baltimore, Maryland, in 1803, and the happy couple visited Niagara Falls on their wedding trip. But wedded bliss was short-lived. Their marriage was annulled two years later. Jerome went on to become the king of Westphalia, in Germany, and later marshal of France.

Businesses in Niagara Falls cater to the thousands of newlyweds who visit each year, giving them special souvenirs or certificates for free admissions. The mists and rainbows have become the background of millions of wedding album photos. You'll see lots of signs advertising cupid specials for newlyweds.

9 *See the night lights of Niagara* — Tourists have always been attracted to the illumination of the Falls. The Falls were first lit up in 1860, the evening before the great performer Blondin walked a tightrope across the gorge to entertain a special visitor, the Prince of Wales. Today during the regular tourist season the waters are illuminated every night. More than 24 multicolored searchlights, each nearly 3 feet (1 meter) in diameter, play on the Falls. A special Festival of Lights is held from November through February. During the Festival, many of the trees, parks and buildings are bathed in seasonal colors for the holidays. Christmas lights are strung from the top to the bottom of the Skylon Tower, making it into the world's largest Christmas tree!

10 *Send a postcard* — There are over 5,000 different postcard views of Niagara Falls. A trip to any antique market or secondhand store can get you a handful of different postcards, some from long ago. Modern postcard racks are filled with artistic views of the Falls. Be sure to write "Yours till Niagara Falls" on the postcard!

11 *Climb a tower* — The Minolta Tower (formerly the Panasonic Tower) stands 660 feet (200 meters) above the Niagara Gorge and has three open observation levels. Tourists can watch "The Waltzing Water," a sight and sound show in the tower coordinated to the movement of water from 972 water jets. There is also an aquarium and a reptile exhibit at the tower.

The Skylon Tower is 775 feet (235 meters) above the Falls. It has indoor and outdoor observation decks. From the ground, the yellow elevators on the outside of the tower look like insects. Observation towers on the Canadian and American sides of the river enable you to see the Falls from many different angles.

12 *Go ghostbusting: visit a fort* — A short drive from Niagara Falls will take you to Fort Erie, Fort George or Fort Niagara. Watch for the ghost of the soldier at Fort Niagara. Try a bed for size at Fort Niagara: you'll find adults were much shorter 200 years ago. Imagine living in the enclosures during the winter months. Blustery winds from the river and Lake Ontario make even a summer visit a chilly one.

13 *List some anagrams* — An anagram is a word or phrase formed when you rearrange some or all of the letters of another word. Take the words NIAGARA FALLS and write as many anagrams as you can. Here are a few to get you started: flair, grain, fall, alas, Alan, snail, ring. Remember, you may use each letter only as often as it appears in NIAGARA FALLS, so you can't use *I* more than once, but you have four *A*s and two *L*s. At least 90 words and names can be created — good luck!

14 *Walk through a garden* — Everywhere you walk near the Falls is overflowing with beautiful flowers. Each April, Queen Victoria Park is filled with nodding bright yellow daffodils; in fact, there are so many flowers that the park has become known as "the daffodil

capital of North America." Spring brings out millions of tulips, and in the early summer the Centennial Lilac Gardens, near the Lewiston-Queenston Bridge, are abloom with more than 1,200 lilac bushes.

The Niagara Parks School of Horticulture plants and maintains the gorgeous gardens and shrubs in the Niagara Falls area. Graduates from the school go on to work for other towns and cities. When you wander through the Oakes Garden Theatre, on the site of the old Clifton Hotel, ask one of the gardeners about the unusual plants you see. Your trip to Niagara Falls could end up being an interesting botany lesson.

Don't miss the Greenhouse, located near Table Rock House. All year round there are exhibitions of plants for every season.

15 *Generate some electricity* — A trip to Power Vista, the New York Power Authority's building at the Robert Moses Power Plant, is well worth the time. There you can see short films that explain hydro-electricity. You can see how power is transmitted in a gigantic diorama, complete with running water. You can even generate electricity yourself by pumping water into a turbine. When you stand on the glass bridge at Power Vista you are as close as you can be to the huge generators.

16 *Set your watch* — by the Floral Clock. Near the Sir Adam Beck – Niagara Generating Station No. 1 you can see the 85-foot (26-meter) face of the clock, which is planted with 19,000 plants each year. All the plants are grown in the Niagara Parks Greenhouse. A pool with a water garden in it surrounds the clock, which strikes every quarter-hour. The first clock was built in 1950; it was modelled on a similar clock in Edinburgh, Scotland.

17 *Cross the Whirlpool Rapids* — Take a ride on the Spanish Aero Car. The car, originally built in 1916 by a Spanish company, moves 250 feet (76 meters) above the waters of the Whirlpool. Today the car is lighter, the engines operating it have been updated, and the landing platforms have been made safer. This is the best way to view the raging whirlpool and its rapids.

18 *Climb to Clifton Hill* — When the sun goes down, the people come out to stroll through the Clifton Hill section of Niagara Falls. There you can buy a T-shirt or food from street vendors, play miniature golf or just people-watch. Buildings such as Maple Leaf Village boast about their attractions, like the Elvis Presley Museum, and their arcades. You can visit the Houdini Hall of Fame (Houdini never visited Niagara Falls), the Ripley's Believe-It-or-Not Museum or the Louis Tussaud Wax Museum. Everything is very noisy and lit with neon lights — a street-stroller's delight.

19 *Tunnel under the Falls* — You'll be given a raincoat when you go into the Scenic Tunnels under Table Rock House. You end up behind the Horseshoe Falls, listening to the roar of the water. Or you can stand at the foot of the Falls on an observation platform. On the American side you can visit the Cave of the Winds. There too you will be given a slicker to wear. You can climb along a walkway that leads to the base of Bridal Veil Falls.

20 *Sketch Niagara Falls* — If you've brought along a pad of paper, do as thousands of amateur and professional artists have done through the centuries and sketch a picture of the Falls. You don't even have to be accurate — the first picture was drawn by someone who hadn't even been there! Just try to capture the awesome volume of the waterfalls. Your memories will fill in the rest of the sound and color better than any postcard or photograph.

CHAPTER 2
Adventurers All

The Maid of the Mist

T HE word Niagara comes from the Indian word "onguiaahra," which means the throat or the strait. Some historians say the word also means the thunderer. Try saying "onguiaahra" many times out loud — does it sound at all like Niagara?

Long ago, the Niagara River was an important trade route for the Indians in the region. The area around the Falls was settled by the Neutrals, an Indian tribe that remained neutral in the wars between the Hurons to the north and the Iroquois to the south. The Neutrals were gentle people who believed in the powers of gods who commanded the wind, the rain and the sun. Hinu was the Great Thunderer who, the Neutrals claimed, lived in a cave behind the waterfalls. This made Niagara Falls a sacred place for the Neutrals.

Today you can travel under the Falls on a tourist boat called *The Maid of the Mist*. The boats were named after an Indian princess. This is her story.

Sickness had befallen an Indian village. To stop the sickness, the people decided to sacrifice Lelawalo, the daughter of the chief, to please Hinu. She was put into a canoe and left to drift over the edge of the Falls to her death. But Hinu's sons took pity on the brave Lelawalo. After she fell over the Falls they told her spirit what was causing the sickness in the village: an evil serpent that lived in the river was poisoning the people's water.

Lelawalo's spirit returned to her village and told the people how to save themselves. The villagers attacked the serpent, and it returned to the river to die. According to legend, the serpent twisted into a curved shape as it died, and that shape became the Horseshoe Falls.

The peaceful Neutrals were eventually killed or captured by the fiercer Indian nations surrounding them, and the area was later settled by the Mississauga and Seneca tribes. Some people claim you can still see Lelawalo, her long hair flowing, rising from the mists at the bottom of the Falls.

EXPLORERS AND TRADERS

The Niagara River was like a great water highway from Lake Ontario to Lake Erie and on into the unknown territories to the west. But the waterfalls made it impossible to travel all the way by water. To get around the Falls, the Indians created a 9-mile (14.4-kilometer) portage.

The portage was a difficult one. At one point, near today's Artpark in Lewiston, New York, the trail became so steep that portagers loaded with 80-pound (36-kilogram) packs had to crawl on their hands and knees. Not surprisingly, this place was known as "Crawl-on-All-Fours."

No one knows who was the very first European visitor to Niagara Falls. Some early visitors included explorers and traders and the priests who travelled with them. The first eyewitness account of Niagara Falls was recorded in 1678 by Father Louis Hennepin, a priest from the Spanish Netherlands. He was travelling with an advance party for the French explorer La Salle.

If you lived in Europe at that time and could read (many people could not), this is what you would have learned from Father Hennepin about Niagara Falls:

> Four leagues* from Lake Frontenac there is an incredible Cataract or Waterfall, which has no equal. The Niagara River near this place is only the eighth of a league wide, but it is very deep in places, and so rapid above the great fall that it hurries down all the animals which try to cross it, without a single one being able to withstand its current. They plunge down a height of more than five hundred feet, and its fall is composed of two sheets of water and a cascade, with an island sloping down. In the middle these waters foam and boil in a fearful manner.

Hennepin's description led Europeans to believe that the Falls were more than 500 feet (152 meters) high and that the roar of the waterfalls could be heard from 45 miles (72 kilometers) away. Today we know that the falls he drew (the American Falls) are actually about 190 feet (58 meters) high. No wonder Father Hennepin came to be called *le grand menteur*, "the great liar."

* A league is a unit of distance equal to about 3 miles (5 kilometers). Perhaps you've read the fairy tale about Seven League Boots or Jules Verne's *Twenty-thousand Leagues Under the Sea*.

The Big Picture

Father Hennepin's exaggerated description of Niagara Falls appeared in a book along with a picture of the Falls by an unknown artist. This inaccurate picture, drawn from Father Hennepin's description, was the first ever published of the Falls and made the priest's tales seem true.

The picture was reprinted for more than a hundred years, until North American painters actually went to the Falls and painted what they saw. Imagine painting a picture of the Rocky Mountains if you were given all the wrong measurements!

Pag. 22 Part. 1.st

AN EXPLORER PLAGUED BY TRAGEDY

One of the earliest explorers to visit the Falls was René-Robert Cavalier, Sieur de La Salle. La Salle had come to New France in 1666 and quickly became interested in exploration and fur trading. By 1679 he had made his way to the Niagara River. He ordered his followers to build Fort Conté on the east bank of the river. (Today it is the site of Fort Niagara.) Tragedy No. 1: Fort Conté was destroyed by fire and abandoned.

Near the mouth of today's Cayuga Creek, La Salle's hardworking crew also built a ship called the *Griffon*, which became the first boat larger than a canoe to travel on the upper Great Lakes. Tragedy No. 2: the ship was lost in a storm in 1679.

La Salle claimed the Niagara region for France. After he left the Falls area, he continued to explore North America. He became the first European to follow the Mississippi River to its mouth. In 1682, he claimed the surrounding territory for France and named it Louisiana, to honor King Louis XIV of France. But there in the swamps, in 1687, La Salle's final tragedy occurred: his weary, angry men killed him. The Indian prophecy of years before came true.

FORTS AND BATTLES

The French and British battled fiercely to establish their claim to North America. And the Indians fought both groups in an attempt to hold on to their land. One encounter, the Devil's Hole Massacre, became famous.

Pontiac, chief of the western Ottawas tribe, had been promised by the British that no Europeans would settle or hunt along the Niagara River. Instead, the British said, the area would be maintained as a trading center and a military stronghold. But that promise was broken in 1763: Europeans hunted and settled where they pleased. Several hundred angry Senecas ambushed a British wagon train and its military escort. The attack took place at a point along the portage route called Devil's Hole, near today's Robert Moses Power Plant.

SIEUR de LA SALLE

A WARNING FOR LA SALLE

According to Indian legend, the explorer La Salle was warned about his ill-fated future during his time in the Niagara region. An Iroquois chief named Gironkouthie took the explorer into the Devil's Hole cave to hear the voice of Hinu, the god of the Falls. According to the chief, Hinu warned that if La Salle travelled farther south he would meet death. Hinu was right. Years later, when La Salle explored the region at the mouth of the Mississippi River, he was killed by his own men.

A SOLDIER'S GEAR

Visits to restored forts in both the United States and Canada can make you feel like you have gone back in time, hundreds of years ago. Historical interpreters (the people who work at the museums and forts) are often dressed in clothing of the period and are glad to tell you about day-to-day life.

At Fort Niagara, New York, young men are dressed in uniforms identical to those worn by members of the King's Eighth Regiment of Foot, 200 years ago.

Their heavy wool jackets, red with royal blue facings, are very hot during the summer. (A facing is a strip of material sewn to the edge of a jacket to make it stronger and to decorate it.) Long ago, the jacket was never washed because the dye would run. (Today it can be dry-cleaned.) With its trim and buttons, a jacket weighs 14 pounds (6.4 kilograms).

A leather stock, a sort of collar, is worn around the neck for two reasons: to keep the soldier's posture straight while he is marching and to keep him from falling asleep while he is on watch. The stock is stiff and uncomfortable.

The socks are woolen, as are the breeches.

A nightshirt, which hangs to the knees, is worn at all times. Soldiers long ago slept in it at night and tucked it into their breeches in the morning.

A soldier wears a vest and his hat.

Finally, the soldier carries a British "Brown Bess" rifle, which weighs 14 pounds (6.4 kilograms).

Imagine yourself in 1780, dressed in all this unwashed, heavy clothing, marching on a hot, humid August day.

Soldiers at Fort Niagara heard the screams of the Senecas and the ambushed men. They hurried to help, only to find themselves surrounded too. Two days after the attack, British soldiers found the bodies of more than 80 men, scalped and lying on the trail. Many more bodies and broken wagons lay in the Niagara Gorge. Few escaped. One survivor, John Stedman, was the wagonmaster of the group. His grazing goats later gave Goat Island its name.

The brutality of the ambush turned many people against Chief Pontiac. In 1764, at an Indian council held at Fort Niagara, the British commander, Sir William Johnson, demanded that the Indians give up their claims to the Niagara portage route. To keep peace in the area the British built Fort Erie (in 1764) and Fort George (in 1796).

SETTLING IN

When the American Revolution started in 1775, many Loyalists (people who remained loyal to the British king) fled from the American colonies to Canada. They did not want to break away from Britain as other Americans did; they wanted "Unity of Empire" and so were called "United Empire Loyalists."

Many Loyalists who lived in New York fled to the Niagara area for safety. Fort Niagara, still in the hands of the British, provided shelter for the Loyalists and their Indian allies, who had lost their lands and belongings when they fled.

The Loyalists soon began to build their own homes near the Falls. They planted fruit trees and tenderly nurtured them. Those trees are the grandparents of today's Niagara Peninsula orchards.

The east bank of the Niagara River was given to the United States after the American Revolution. The west bank, where many of the Loyalists settled, remained under the rule of Quebec until the creation of the province of Upper Canada in 1791.

Goodbye, France!

After a long, hard battle, the French surrendered Fort Niagara, located where the Niagara River meets Lake Ontario, to the British on July 25, 1759. France lost *all* claims to Canadian territories (then called New France) at the end of the Seven Years' War in 1763.

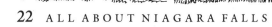

THE FIVE INDIAN NATIONS

The story of Niagara Falls in the early days involved the Five Indian Nations. These were five tribes (nations) of Iroquois linked by language and culture. They were also known as the League of the Iroquois. From western to eastern New York, they were:

Senecas	meaning	People of the Mountain and Keeper of the Western Gate
Cayugas	meaning	People of the Swan
Onondagas	meaning	People of the Hills
Oneidas	meaning	People of the Upright Stone
Mohawks	meaning	People of the Flint and Keeper of the Eastern Gate

They were joined in the 1750s by the **Tuscaroras** (meaning Weavers of the Shirt), who came from North Carolina. Together, these tribes formed the Six Nations. Some of their descendants live at the Six Nations Reserve near Brantford, Ontario.

If you look at a map of New York State, you can easily find five of the six nations in the names of cities, towns, rivers, lakes and a valley. Can you tell which Indian nation is missing?

At Fort Niagara, New York, you can see the Gate of the Five Nations (Porte des Cinq Nations) as you enter. The gate was built in 1756 and named to honor the Iroquois nations. The officials also thought that the Indians would be less likely to attack them after this friendly gesture. Friendly or not, the gate was built as a fortification as well.

The Niagara Escarpment is visible 6 miles (9.6 kilometers) upstream at Lewiston, New York. Sometimes you can also see a plume of mist rising above the Falls, 13 miles (21 kilometers) away.

The French Thorns

When you visit Fort George, look for the hawthorn bushes located on the Niagara Parkway, south of the fort. It is said that the original piece of thorn from which these grew can be traced back to the bush on Golgotha from which Christ's crown of thorns was made.

According to legend, Pope Clement brought a branch from the Holy Land and planted it near the cathedral in Avignon, France. Some say Crusaders brought the thorns to France. Missionaries to New France then took branches with them and planted thorns in the garrison towns they visited.

A recent study reports that the thorns are an Old World species that can be found growing nowhere else in North America. The bushes at Fort George are 10 feet (3 meters) high and the thorns are a nasty 3 inches (8 centimeters) long.

Life in a Fort

At Fort Erie, Ontario, visitors are given a good idea of what a soldier's barracks and family life were like.

Soldiers slept on straw-filled palliasses (thin mattresses) with head bolsters (hard pillows), coarse, scratchy linen sheets and heavy wool blankets. Each bunk held more than one soldier.

At night, the fireplaces and candles gave weak light and much smoke. The sleeping quarters were filled to overflowing with people.

During peacetime, six wives per company were allowed to accompany their husbands, and any children under the age of 14 were given rations and accommodation. Imagine the noise.

There was little privacy for families in the quarters. A mother might hang up a blanket or sheet to make a room divider for a bit of family privacy, but extra blankets were hard to come by.

Soldiers, their families and doctors often wrote of how dirty, crowded and unhealthy the soldiers' quarters were. Can you imagine being one of those children of the fort?

The Ghost of Fort Niagara

Nothing's better on a dark night full of wind and scratching branches than a ghost story. This one features a ghost that's hundreds of years old.

During the time the French controlled Fort Niagara (before 1759), two French officers argued about a Seneca woman whom they both fancied. They challenged each other to a duel with swords. In the vestibule of the castle within the fort, near the open well that supplied the residents with drinking water, the two passionate soldiers fought until one was killed. The victor cut off the head of the slain soldier and threw it into Lake Ontario, and he pushed the body down the well. No one else knew about the duel.

After the British took control of the fort in 1759, the British commander, Sir William Johnson, ordered the well sealed. He feared that the departing French soldiers might have poisoned the water supply as their revenge upon the British.

Many years passed and the fort fell into ruins. Then historians decided to restore it. They found the original plans for Fort Niagara in Paris. The restorers unsealed the well, and ever since then, when the moon is full, people at the fort have claimed to see the ghost roaming the castle, searching for his head!

CHAPTER 3

War!

EACH day thousands of people walk, bike and drive across the Peace Bridge over the Niagara River to visit Canada or the United States. The border between the two countries is halfway across the bridge.

The border wasn't always as peaceful as it is today. In 1812, for example, the United States declared war on Great Britain. The Americans felt the British were interfering in their affairs. They were particularly upset about Britain's treatment of American citizens at sea. A British ship would pull alongside an American ship, and its sailors would come aboard. They claimed they were searching for British naval deserters. Then they kidnapped, or "impressed," male passengers and forced them to serve in the British navy.

Since Canada was under British control, the Americans naturally directed most of their attacks to the border area.

A Bridge for Peace
The Peace Bridge was built in 1927 and named to commemorate more than 100 years of peace on the Niagara frontier. The Niagara River is a part of the shared international boundary that is called "the longest undefended border in the world."

THE BATTLE OF QUEENSTON HEIGHTS

One of the most famous battles in the War of 1812 was the Battle of Queenston Heights, fought on October 13, 1812. On that autumn day, American Major-General Stephen Van Rensselaer crossed into Canada from Lewiston, New York, with 4,000 men and captured the heights. British General Sir Isaac Brock arrived from Fort George, the main British fort on the Niagara frontier, and tried to retake them.

Cannons thundered across the gorge, from Fort Niagara on the American side and Fort George on the Canadian side. Brock was killed in battle that afternoon, but his replacement, Major-General Roger Hale Sheaffe, with the help of Indians, eventually recaptured the heights. The Americans raised the white flag and surrendered.

James Secord, in peacetime a storekeeper, was wounded during the Battle of Queenston Heights. His wife, Laura, looked for her husband among the dead and wounded on the mountain and took him home to recover. One year later Laura Secord became a hero.

LAURA SECORD'S WALK

Laura Secord was born in Great Barrington, Massachusetts, and moved with her family, the Ingersolls, to Upper Canada in 1795. She and her family lived in the village of Queenston.

During the war, the Secords and others had to provide food and shelter on demand to the enemy. One night Laura overheard a startling conversation between American soldiers at her dinner table. They were discussing an attack on the British, planned for the next week. Laura decided to warn the British commander.

On June 22, 1813, Laura left her house at 4:30 in the morning to warn Lieutenant James Fitzgibbon and his troops 20 miles (32 kilometers) away. It had rained all the night before, so the ground was soggy and the day was very hot and sticky.

Fearing she would be captured by the Americans or the Indians, Laura had a handy excuse for her trip. She put on

Laura Secord walked to DeCew house to warn Fitzgibbon.

LAURA SECORD'S COW

History books and paintings have shown Laura Secord and her cow as partners on the historic walk. But the truth is, there never was a cow. Historians have recently discovered that Laura Secord herself never mentioned a cow, nor did any member of her family. It appears the cow story began in 1864 when historian William Coffin began to treat Laura like a heroine: he trimmed the true story with a few extras, which became accepted as accurate details. In 1913 she was chosen as the name and symbol for a Canadian candy company. On each box is a portrait of Laura — without her cow.

"visiting" clothes and packed a basket. If anyone asked, she would claim she was going to visit her sick brother in St. David's. Sturdy boots would have been useful for the hike, but they surely would have given her away to the enemy. Her niece, Elizabeth Secord, came part of the way with her but was unable to continue because of her poor health.

Laura walked on through the muddy Black Swamp, encountering Mohawk guards who let her pass. Some Indians accompanied her on the last part of her journey. She arrived in the evening, exhausted by the effort, the heat and her fear. Fitzgibbon already knew that the Americans had plans to attack, but Laura Secord's efforts were still heroic. She had put the good of her country before her own safety and comfort.

Two days later, the Americans were ambushed by the Indians and the British, and they surrendered. Laura returned to her family. Fitzgibbon and the Secords told no one about her heroic journey. They didn't want the Americans to find out and retaliate. Her story was not generally known until it was first published in 1845.

Laura died in 1868 at age 93, a poor, unrecognized heroine of Upper Canada. She was buried next to her husband in Drummond Hill Cemetery, in Niagara Falls, Ontario. The cemetery ground was once the scene of what became known as the fiercest and bloodiest battle of the War of 1812 — the Battle of Lundy's Lane.

LUNDY'S LANE

Lundy's Lane is only blocks away from the Falls. It was named after William Lundy, a Quaker from Pennsylvania who was granted land in the area at the end of the American Revolution. There were orchards nearby but not many houses. Back then, meadows and heavily wooded areas still existed very close to the Falls.

July was a month of heavy fighting between the enemies. The Americans captured Fort Erie early in July and defeated the British at the Battle of Chippawa on July 5, as they marched toward the Falls. The troops burned St. David's on July 19 and then moved back to a ridge at Lundy's Lane. On July 25, the

American and British troops arrived. There, within earshot of the Falls, the fighting began. It started at dinnertime and lasted until midnight. Some troops had marched 20 miles (32 kilometers) that day and were tired when they arrived to fight. For three hours they fought hand to hand in total darkness, not knowing if they were killing friend or foe.

No one really won the battle. The Canadians and the British saw it as their victory; the Americans claimed *they* had won. American Major-General Jacob Brown left the field when his soldiers were too exhausted to continue fighting. Likewise, Lieutenant-General Gordon Drummond and his British troops could fight no longer and withdrew from Lundy's Lane. A doctor who went to the battle scene later saw more than 70 horses dead and more than 1,000 soldiers wounded or dead on the field. As the American troops left, they threw cannons and other heavy equipment into the rapids above the Falls. They also ruined the bridge at Chippawa as they retreated to Fort Erie. The bodies of dead soldiers and the wooden fenceposts surrounding the area were piled on the field and burned. Local legend said that grass would not grow on that spot for years afterward.

For nearly 50 years the Lundy's Lane battlefield was a popular tourist attraction, second only to the Falls. Observation towers were built, and visitors were charged 25 cents in 1846 to climb up and view the field. But gradually people lost interest in the battle site. Lundy's Lane was neglected and became an overgrown field. Many years later the battlefield was cleaned up and marked with a monument recognizing the losses of the British and Canadian forces on that hot July evening.

The War of 1812, like the Battle of Lundy's Lane, had no real winner. Towns, bridges and people's lives had been destroyed, and in the end no one was victorious. Great Britain and the United States sent representatives to Ghent, Belgium, and there, on Christmas Eve, 1814, they signed a treaty to end the war. The Treaty of Ghent did not discuss any of the issues that had been so important before the war. Everything was to be *status quo ante bellum*, or "as it was before the war." Lands that had been captured were returned to their original owners. But the War of 1812 wasn't the last time Americans fought British and Canadians near the Falls....

Sir Isaac Brock's Many Burials

The body of Sir Isaac Brock was buried at Fort George on October 16, 1812. Captain John Macdonell, who had died in battle with Brock, was buried with him. But Brock and Macdonell were not allowed to rest in peace.

Twelve years later, they were moved to a vault under the monument at Queenston Heights. In 1840 the monument was nearly destroyed by an explosion and Brock and Macdonell were removed and buried again in a private cemetery below the heights in Queenston. In 1856, the bodies of the two men reached their final resting place, this time in a vault below the new Queenston Heights monument, the one you see now when you visit the heights.

Living Through the War

During the war people suffered many hardships. Villages and towns and crops were burned to the ground. The men were away fighting or were captured as prisoners of war. When enemy troops approached, the women had to gather their children and as many belongings as they could and leave quickly. People sometimes had to flee so fast that they were barefoot in the snow and had no food or fuel. The lucky ones were able to bury their valuables; others lost everything they owned.

The women proved strong and dependable. Some helped in battle, passing ammunition and loading guns. They tended the wounded. Many women took over all the daily farming chores and other work that the absent men would have done. Work included the production of potash, a major export of the area. Potash

was made by boiling wood ashes and water in large iron pots over outdoor fires. When the water had all evaporated, the potash was left behind. Much of the potash was shipped to England, where it was used to make crystals for chandeliers, soap, dyes and ceramics.

CHAPTER 4

Snapshots from History

THE crackle of gunfire was heard many times near Niagara Falls until nearly 1870. People living nearby sometimes found themselves in the middle of yet another conflict, with little warning. If you put together an album of these tense historical moments you could include these events.

THE *CAROLINE* AND THE 1837 REBELLION

On the night of December 29, 1837, a ship called the *Caroline* teetered at the brink of the Falls. Fires raged below decks, and as the fast-moving Niagara River swept the ship over the Falls, explosions ripped apart its hull.

Why did the *Caroline* go over the Falls? It all began with the editor of the *Colonial Advocate*, William Lyon Mackenzie. Mackenzie hated the leaders of the Upper Canada government, and he filled his paper with attacks against them.

William Lyon Mackenzie

On December 5, 1837, Mackenzie and about 700 followers met at Montgomery's Tavern on Yonge Street, north of Toronto, and planned to attack Toronto and overthrow the government of Upper Canada. The rebellion failed, and Mackenzie and his rebels were chased to Niagara Falls.

Mackenzie didn't give up. He set up camp on Navy Island and proclaimed himself the chief of state of the Republic of Canada. He had his own flag, with two stars representing French and British Canada, and even began to print his own money.

Mackenzie and his followers got weapons and supplies from Fort Schlosser in New York State. The supplies were smuggled to the rebels on board the *Caroline*. The ship had made several successful trips, but on the night of December 29, 1837, her luck ran out. Colonel Allan MacNab, the Canadian commander at Fort Chippawa, became suspicious as the ship sailed by and ordered some of his soldiers to board the *Caroline* and take it over. The ship's watchman was killed in the scuffle. The rest of the crew were put ashore. Fires were started below decks, and the ship was left to drift into the middle of the Niagara River. Over the Falls it went.

The rebel Mackenzie fled to Grand Island and then to Rochester, New York. There he was jailed for urging Americans to make war on Canada, but he was eventually pardoned. Mackenzie returned to Upper Canada, was elected to Parliament and remained an outspoken radical. His grandson, William Lyon Mackenzie King, became prime minister of Canada in the 1920s.

THE UNDERGROUND RAILROAD

Imagine yourself, in 1861, a mistreated slave in South Carolina. You've been abused, overworked, taken from your family, treated worse than the family pet. You have no rights and maybe no name. Desperate, you'll risk your life for the freedom others take for granted. You run away.

Moving only at night, in darkness and in fear, you travel north. If you're lucky, you won't be captured by bounty hunters — you'll make it to the northern states or into Canada.

Although there had been slavery in Upper Canada as late as 1793, Lieutenant-Governor John Graves Simcoe and the legislature passed a bill that called for the gradual abolition of slavery, and by 1815 slavery in Upper Canada was nearly gone.

But slavery continued to grow in the United States, and during the American Civil War (1861-1865) certain places along the Canadian border became "stations" along an "underground railroad." This railroad had no real trains and was not underground. It earned its name because of the swift and quiet way in which runaway slaves were moved to freedom. The slaves travelled at night and hid during the day. Hiding places were called "stations," and the people who aided the slaves were called "conductors."

Many of the routes from the northern states passed through Niagara Falls, New York, before ending in southern Ontario. Some reports claimed that as many as 200 slaves arrived in Upper Canada each week.

Uncle Tom

American writer Harriet Beecher Stowe visited Niagara Falls when she was researching her novel *Uncle Tom's Cabin* (1851). The model for the character Uncle Tom was the Reverend Josiah Henson, who smuggled runaway slaves across the Niagara River into Canada. Stowe and Henson met in Lockport, New York, where he told her about his anti-slavery work. His home was outside Dresden, Ontario, about 150 miles (240 kilometers) south-west of Niagara Falls. There he established a black community and the British American Institute, Canada's first vocational school. At the school, runaway slaves could live safely and learn manual trades.

Uncle Tom's Cabin was a powerful book that made people more aware of the evils of slavery. Henson's home and grave, as well as six museum buildings, are located about a mile west of Dresden.

Upper and Lower Canada

In 1791 Britain divided the area known as Quebec into two areas. Lower Canada was the southern portion of present-day Quebec, divided from Upper Canada by the Ottawa River. Most residents of Lower Canada were French-speaking. Upper Canada was what we now call Ontario; it was settled largely by Americans and English-speaking Europeans.

In 1841 the Act of Union, passed in Britain, united Upper and Lower Canada into the Province of Canada.

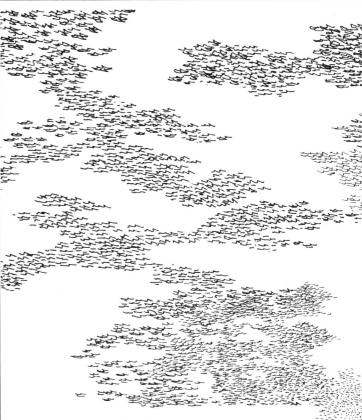

The Pigeons of Niagara

Janet Carnochan was one of the first writers to research Niagara Falls history. In her book *The History of Niagara*, published in 1914, she includes this story: "In 1847 and 1848 we are told of flocks of pigeons in such numbers that the light was obscured. On a Sunday in March a flock described as a mile wide and one hundred and sixty miles long, took over four hours, from 7:30 to 12 o'clock noon to fly over the town. Sometimes they flew so low that they were killed by the boys with clubs. Remarkable tales are told of the number killed with one shot, ranging from seven to forty...."

Anyone for pigeon pie?

THE FENIAN RAIDS

The summer air was filled with the heavy smell of smoking rifles as the Fenians, Irish-Americans who wanted Ireland's independence from Britain, clashed with Canadian soldiers at Ridgeway, Ontario, on June 2, 1866. Curious residents of Niagara Falls paid a fee and watched the battle from the observation towers at Lundy's Lane. They got their money's worth of action.

The Fenians were nearly 10,000 American Civil War veterans, outfitted with Civil War gear, who carried out raids in both the United States and Canada. Although the group defeated the Canadians at Ridgeway, the Fenian movement soon collapsed. The Upper Canada government, led by Sir John A. Macdonald, feared that more attacks by the Americans would lead to another war. The government's action to strengthen the provinces resulted in unification and the Confederation of Canada in 1867.

THE NIAGARA KITE CONTEST

Early in 1848, American Charles Ellett was hired to build a bridge across the Niagara River. He had a problem, however. How could he get the first cable 700 feet (213 meters) across the river? The waters, especially near the Whirlpool Rapids, were too fast-moving to swim through, and no one could throw a cable across the wide gorge.

Ellett decided to have a kite-flying contest and "fly" the cable across. The first boy to get a kite from the American to the Canadian side would receive a $10 prize. (Remember, $10 then was worth a great deal more than it is now!)

On the first day of the contest no one won, but the second day an American boy named Homan Walsh flew his kite over to the Canadian side of the river. Attached to

the kite string was a lightweight rope. It was used to pull a heavier rope across the gorge. Then that rope pulled an even heavier rope, and so on until finally a steel cable was pulled across to the Canadian side.

The contractors had succeeded in the first step of their bridge-building, thanks to a boy and his kite.

Ellett's bridge opened in July 1848. It was followed by the first successful suspension railway bridge in the world, built by John Roebling and opened in 1855.

CHAPTER 5

Come See the Falls

MORE than 12 million tourists visit Niagara Falls each year, some on holiday visits, others as honeymooners and still others simply curious. Today you can watch the spectacle from the safety of the park look-outs. Or, if you're daring, you can take a ride under the Falls on one of the *Maid of the Mist* boats. Two hundred years ago, sightseeing at Niagara Falls was much more dangerous. Travellers were taken by guides down ladders leaning against the gorge walls. They had to scramble over rocks and brush to see the caverns behind the Falls. There were no railings or retaining walls.

The first visitors had only the natural power and beauty of the waterfalls to hypnotize them, but later tourists were lured by extra entertainments. People quickly discovered that there was money to be made from curious visitors. Tourists needed places to stay overnight. And they needed places to eat and other sights to see after they had had their fill of the Falls. They might want souvenirs to take home to prove they had been to the Falls — some petrified mist, perhaps, or Indian crafts not made by Indians at all.

Before 1850 you could walk out onto Table Rock, with no fences to protect you.

The same place in 1924. Jutting Table Rock has fallen off, and there are now protective fences.

The longer the visitors stayed at Niagara Falls, the more money they could be convinced to spend, and there were plenty of slick "businessmen" to help them spend every penny.

There were taverns on both sides of the river. Hotels quickly sprang up along the Canadian side of the Falls, just beyond what was called the Chain Reserve. This reserve was a strip of land 66 feet (20 meters) wide along the edge of the river. It was set aside by the government to give troops access to military outposts along the river in times of emergency.

Early tourists wrote about the carnival atmosphere of the Canadian side of the Falls. If you visited in the mid-1800s, you might be approached by a number of "characters": men trying to convince you to stay at a particular inn (they would receive a commission), pickpockets working the tourists as they jostled to get the best view and hurdy-gurdy men with dancing monkeys. There would also be hucksters with phony souvenirs of the Falls, beggars, sellers of illegal alcohol, young men calling to crowds from in front of museums and shops, luring you in to come see, come buy.

There were plenty of sideshows and curiosities. There were pagodas to climb (only 25 cents) for a better view of the Falls and pestering peddlers selling just about anything. You could have your picture taken in front of the Falls or, better yet, in front of a painted backdrop of the Falls in a stuffy back room. As early as 1830 visitors complained about the badgering by unsavory types. The street noise must have equalled the roar of the mighty Falls.

Until 1886, when the Statue of Liberty was erected, the Falls at Niagara were the symbol of America and the New World for visitors from the rest of the world. Everyone wanted to see the Falls; a trip to America wasn't complete until you'd been there and felt the mist on your face.

There always seemed to be something exciting going on. Famous people often visited. If you were there on the right day, you might have seen Abraham Lincoln or Charles Dickens or the Prince of Wales. One hotel owner tried to rope off the section of the Chain Reserve in front of his hotel and charged an "admission fee" to see the Falls. The government quickly put an end to this robbery.

In an effort to clean up the rowdiness and cheap carnival atmosphere on "the Front," as the main street was called, the Ontario government bought the land and demolished the run-down buildings. A growing pride in the natural beauty of the area and a desire to protect that beauty led the government to establish Queen Victoria Park, Canada's first provincial park, in 1887. The town's other attractions moved up to the Clifton Hill area, where you find them today. Preserving the natural beauty of the Falls area is still the main job of the Niagara Parks Commission.

The Falls themselves seemed to cooperate in "putting on a good show" for the tourists. From time to time, something spectacular would happen. In 1850, for example, Table Rock, a ledge of rock on the Canadian side, broke off. A man washing his horse-drawn cab there jumped to safety as the ledge and cab fell into the gorge. More than 100 years later, in 1954, the projecting ledge on the American side, called Prospect Point, weighing about 185,000 tons (168,000 tonnes), broke off and fell into the gorge. These dramatic changes to the Falls brought tourists back time and time again.

A Royal Visit
In 1792 the Duke of Kent visited Niagara Falls. There he found one small log hut for visitors, and he went down from Table Rock by way of a "rude, rickety Indian ladder." Sightseeing in those days could be hazardous to your health, and royalty fared no better than the common man at Niagara.

Winter visitors at Prospect Park, 1904.

Would you like to buy some...

Niagara mist
This souvenir "petrified mist" from the Falls was really ordinary stones. Some weren't even local stones — they were imported from England.

Niagara canes
These crook-necked canes, sold as souvenirs, were supposedly made from trees on Navy Island. However, there were never as many trees on the island as there were canes sold.

The whales of Niagara

In 1765, Benjamin Franklin wrote to the editor of a London newspaper: "The grand leap of the whale up the Fall of Niagara is esteemed, by all who have seen it, as one of the finest spectacles of nature." Franklin wrote this to chide the gullible English for their ignorance of America.

My thoughts are strange, magnificent and deep,
When I look down on thee...
Oh what a glorious place for washing sheep
Niagara would be!

Susanna Moodie,
Life in the Clearings, 1853

SAY CHEESE!

Daguerreotypes were all the rage for tourists in the 1850s. These photographs, developed by Frenchman Louis Daguerre, were the result of an impression made on a light-sensitive, silver-coated metallic plate and then developed by mercury vapor. Tourists were posed at the edge of the land above the roaring waters, with their backs to the Falls. A bit risky, to say the least. Later tourists chose to have their souvenir photos taken in front of a painted canvas depicting the Falls. It was safer, but hardly as dramatic as the real thing!

AN ICE BRIDGE

When the temperatures dip low in the winter, the mists and waters at the foot of the Falls freeze, creating a bridge of ice across the river. During the winter months, tourists come by the hundreds to see this natural curiosity. Early photographs and postcards show ladies in long dark dresses and large hats and gentlemen with top hats strolling across the ice bridge. Vendors would set up makeshift shacks in the middle of the ice bridge and sell souvenirs or illegal liquor. When American police came to inspect, the sellers would move their shacks very quickly to the Canadian side of the ice bridge; if Canadian police were inspecting, there was a fast shift back to the American side.

The recreational use of the ice bridge continued until 1912 when three people, a honeymooning couple and a brave man who tried to save them, were caught in the break-up of an ice bridge. They were carried on an ice floe to their death farther down the river. Since then no one has been allowed to go out on the ice bridge.

Danger!!!

In the journals of Mary O'Brien, a young woman who had immigrated to Toronto in the early 1800s, there are a number of interesting entries about her first visit to Niagara Falls. Her description of her walk near the Falls shows just how dangerous a visit could be.

February/March 1832: "We were wet long before we got down, under the guidance of an active young guide, to the lower shelf of land which is on the level of the higher bed of the river. Here we stood on the water's edge just at one angle of the horseshoe. At two paces from our feet the water took its great leap. As we stood on ice and frozen snow, we durst not approach nearer to the brink lest it should break away beneath us."

Mary O'Brien, however, was left a little disappointed. Of the whirlpool she wrote: "It is a curious place, but altogether different and in point of effect inferior to what I had expected." Like many tourists before and after her, Mary had heard so many truer-than-life stories about Niagara Falls that the reality could not measure up to her expectations.

NIAGARAS OF NIAGARAS

Niagara green
Pale green to light bluish-green.

Niagara nose
The name says it all.

Niagarization
This word entered the language when, in the 1850s, trains brought 60,000 visitors a year to Niagara, flooding the area with tourists.

Niagaras of milk
The word Niagara began to be used whenever people spoke of large volumes of liquids.

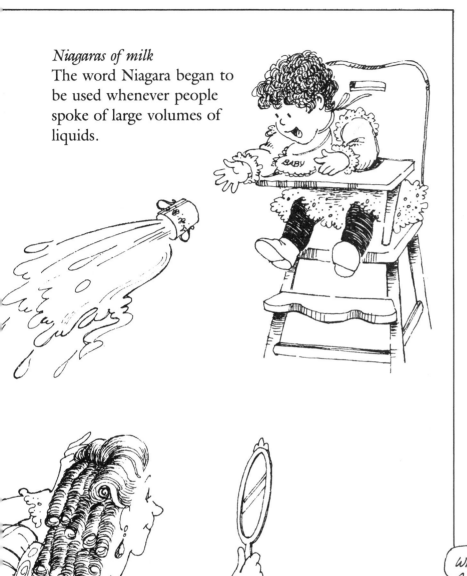

Niagara curls
Also known as cataract curls. This name was given to an 1865 hairstyle: a shower of ringlets that ladies wore at the back of their heads.

WHAT'S THE DIFFERENCE BETWEEN A GIRL'S LONG LOST FRIEND AND THE RAINBOW AT NIAGARA FALLS?

ONE IS MISSED BY THE MAID, THE OTHER IS MADE OF THE MIST!

CHAPTER 6

Over the Falls

WHEN you stand at the Horseshoe Falls the rushing waters thundering over the brink can hypnotize you. For a few seconds you may be afraid. What if you fell? You wouldn't have a chance against the rocks and the current.

On July 9, 1960, seven-year-old Roger Woodward and his teenaged sister Deanne went with an older family friend for a motorboat ride on the Niagara River. The three were enjoying themselves and didn't notice they were entering the rapids above the Falls. By the time they realized that they were in danger, it was too late. The boat's motor was broken, and oars were useless against the current. Quickly the children made sure their lifejackets were tightly fastened. The boat flipped and spilled its passengers into the river.

Screaming, Deanne tried to swim to the shores of Goat Island. Although several tourists watched her struggles, no one moved to help her until she was just 15 feet (4.6 meters) from the edge of the Falls. Then John R. Hayes, a truck driver and auxiliary policeman

from New Jersey, hung from a guardrail by one foot and grabbed Deanne. Another man, John Quattrochi, also from New Jersey, helped Hayes pull the frightened girl to safe ground.

But where was Roger?

While this drama was taking place at the rim of the Falls, down below, the captain of one of the *Maid of the Mist* boats was making his usual trip with a group of tourists. He noticed an orange lifejacket bobbing in the water at the base of the Falls. It was Roger! He had plummeted over the Falls with nothing more to protect him than a lifejacket — and he had survived. Roger was rescued, and despite his horrible fall he had only a few facial bruises. He was indeed a lucky boy. The body of the family friend, James Honeycutt, was found four days later.

Roger and Deanne Woodward became celebrities for a while. And so did Deanne's rescuers. The two men — one black and one white — had worked together to save her. In the racial strife of the 1960s, their heroic cooperative act caught the public's attention.

DRAMA — OR DEATH?

There have never been any guarantees of safety for those who boat or swim above the Falls. But some people seem to have *courted* death as they performed amazing stunts above the Falls or threw themselves over the edge. People have judged some of the stunters to be fools who were greedy for money or fame. But many of the stunters were quite intelligent men and women who could never explain why they took such chances. Some lived; some died terrible deaths.

In the summer of 1985, two men attempted at different times to go over the Falls in barrels. Such stunts have been illegal since 1912. Although both men were fined for their illegal escapades, one tried it again and was successful. The treacherous waters kept him from being rescued for more than an hour; it might have taken days. The manager of the *Maid of the Mist* company said to reporters: "These people who say they have studied the Falls and the river are fools. I have worked the river for 32 years and it's always unpredictable and dangerous. There is no guarantee of that barrel coming out [from under the Falls] at any time."

The unpredictability of nature is what has lured people to see the stunters. Some of the daredevils became sacrifices to mighty Hinu, while others lived to tell their tales.

Francis Abbott, the Hermit of Niagara

In 1830, horrified visitors to Niagara Falls could see a man dangling from, then dancing on, a log stretching from a bridge on Goat Island over the edge of the Horseshoe Falls. The man was Francis Abbott, a hermit who chose to live a lonely existence in a log cabin on Goat Island. Each day he exercised in his unusual way on the log.

One day in the summer of 1831, townspeople found his clothes neatly folded on a ledge near the Falls. Ten days later, the hermit's body was found in the Whirlpool. No clues to his background could be found in his cabin after his death.

Today Abbott's hut is gone, but his story and a place called Hermit's Cave still remain.

A SHIP FULL OF ANIMALS

Stunts at Niagara Falls occurred as early as 1827. In September of that year, a partially dismantled schooner, the *Michigan*, was filled with a menagerie of animals and sent over the Falls. Some claimed only a goose survived. This senseless gimmick was organized by William Forsyth, the owner of the Pavilion, one of the most popular hotels on the Canadian side. William Lyon Mackenzie was an eyewitness and wrote about the stunt for his newspaper, elaborating on the details for added sensationalism. He estimated that 8,000 to 10,000 people were there, hanging from every branch and rooftop, "including show men with wild beasts, gingerbread people, cake and beer stalls, wheel of fortune men, etc." Bands played, people cheered...and a boatload of animals lost their lives.

SAM PATCH

Two years later, even greater crowds came to witness Sam Patch's much-advertised leap into the Falls. The 23-year-old mill worker from Rhode Island was quite a braggart, and he knew how to get the most out of newspaper publicity. He announced he was going to leap nearly 100 feet (30 meters) into the Falls from a tiny platform on Goat Island on October 7, 1829.

The crowds grew still as he paused on the platform. Then, in a patriotic gesture, Sam kissed the American flag and leaped feet first, arms straight by his side. He hit the water at an estimated 60 miles (96 kilometers) per hour, surfaced and swam to the nearby rocks. "There's no mistake in Sam Patch," he said as he climbed from the water. As Sam Patch became more famous, this expression became well known and often used.

A month later, Sam Patch tried another daring leap — this time at the Genesee Falls in New York State. Some observers thought he was a bit shaky before the leap. He seemed in a panic when he fell; he lost control and failed to surface. His body was not found until the next spring and he was buried in a grave near Rochester.

Sam Patch's dramatic death gave America a new folk hero and gave Niagara Falls a stunter to be outdone. Fifteen years

Fact or Fiction?

There are many legends about the American frontiersman Davy Crockett, who supposedly killed a bear when he was only three years old. After his death at the famous battle at the Alamo in Texas, in 1836, many more stories were added. Some people claimed that he once rode *up* Niagara Falls on the back of an alligator!

after his death, children still skipped rope in the schoolyard to a popular jingle:

Poor Sam Patch — a man
    once world renownded,
Much loved the water,
    and by it was drownded.
He sought for fame,
    and as he reached to pluck it,
He lost his ballast, and
    then kicked the buck-it.

BLONDIN THE FUNAMBULIST

In 1859, Jean Francois Gravelet, a well-known French tightrope walker (funambulist), tried an even more amazing stunt. Gravelet was better known as Blondin, or the Prince of Manila. (Manila rope, 2 inches [5 centimeters] thick, was his tightrope material.) On June 30, before a crowd of about 100,000 people, Blondin set out to walk from the American to the Canadian side of the Niagara Gorge across a rope stretched over it. Guy wires attached to the shore helped keep the rope from swaying too much. But the rope, strung 150 feet (46 meters) above the water, sagged in the middle. This meant that part of Blondin's trip would be uphill. The band played the French national anthem as Blondin, carrying his 35-foot (11-meter) balancing pole, stepped onto the rope.

The crowd of watchers on the shore were speechless as Blondin surefootedly scampered across the rope. But many gasped as he sat down on the rope halfway across. To the amazement of all, he lowered a rope to the *Maid of the Mist* below and brought back up a bottle of something to drink. Then he continued his trip across. The entire crossing took only 15 minutes. After celebrating in Canada, he crossed the river, by rope again, but the return trip only took seven minutes!

Blondin made more trips across the gorge during the next year. Each time he thrilled larger crowds with more exciting acts. He balanced a chair on the rope and stood on it. He took pictures of the crowd while he balanced on the rope. He cooked a

BOLD BLONDIN BALANCES BRAVELY ABOVE THE BOILING BREACH

meal on a small portable cooker and lowered it to amazed passengers on the boat below. He crossed while shackled in chains. He crossed carrying his manager on his back, and when the Prince of Wales visited in 1860, Blondin, on stilts, carried his assistant across and performed antics on the way. The prince, like the other spectators, was left breathless and asked Blondin never to do it again. Imagine the prince's reaction when Blondin offered to carry *him* across on his back or in a wheelbarrow!

This French daredevil lived to be 73 years old and died peacefully in his bed, no mean feat for the funambulist who kept crowds gasping as he performed until he was 68.

A FEMALE STUNTER

Women as well as men attempted to make themselves famous by challenging the Falls. On October 24, 1901, Annie Edson Taylor became the first person to go over the Horseshoe Falls in a barrel. Mrs. Taylor was a 43-year-old schoolteacher from Bay City, Michigan, who hoped to become rich and famous by "barrelling" over the Falls. Her escapade was all the more unusual because she couldn't swim. Her oak barrel measured 54 inches (137 centimeters) high and was held together with iron hoops. She was strapped in with leather loops, cushions were placed around her for protection, and air was pumped in to keep her alive.

Launched from the American side, her barrel went over the Falls in ten seconds and drifted to the Canadian side. Rescuers pulled the barrel to shore and opened the lid. There sat Mrs. Taylor, asking if she'd gone over the Falls yet! She had been knocked unconscious and was bleeding from a head wound. She was quick to tell people she wouldn't do it again.

Mrs. Taylor began to call herself "the Queen of the Mist" and started out on a lecture tour to earn money from her stunt. But she did not take her barrel with her, and that's what people wanted to see. The barrel lay rotting in the river. Not many people attended her lectures, so Mrs. Taylor got another barrel and sat beside it in the town of Niagara Falls. She was a sorry sight, trying to tell tourists her story — for a fee, of course.

When she died in 1921, Mrs. Taylor was a pauper without a home. She was buried in Niagara Falls, New York, and her gravestone proclaims her feat, as she did:

Annie Edson Taylor
First to Go Over
The Horseshoe Fall
In a Barrel and Live
October 24, 1901

Other barrel-stunters followed Mrs. Taylor over the Falls, some taking turtles and dogs with them. Sometimes the pets survived and the owners were killed.

Even powerful swimmers were overcome by the raging waters. Captain Matthew Webb of England, who in 1875 became the first swimmer to cross the English Channel, could not succeed at Niagara. Webb's attempt to swim the rapids on July 24, 1883, ended in death when he was sucked into the swirling center of the whirlpool.

Few stunters enjoyed the fame or success they expected after their stunts. If they survived, they returned to the life they had before or died during later stunts. Today people are still unable to explain why they feel they must conquer the mighty, unpredictable, deadly Niagara Falls.

RESCUED BY THE HILL FAMILY

William Hill Sr., nicknamed "Red" because of his tawny hair, was the most famous of the Niagara riverpeople, the people who really know the river and rescue people from it. Hill knew some of the Niagara daredevils and made a number of successful trips himself through the rapids in a barrel.

In August 1918, a dumping scow with two men aboard was marooned in the upper rapids, above the Horseshoe Falls. (A scow is a large flat-bottomed boat with square ends.) Just when it looked as if the men would be carried to their deaths, they managed to ground the scow on some rocks opposite the Toronto powerhouse. If you visit Niagara Falls you will see the scow there.

Red Hill helped rescue the stranded men. A gun was used to shoot a line from the powerhouse to the scow. Then Hill shimmied along the rope over the rapids to the scow. He helped the men back to shore and was later awarded a medal for his efforts.

Hill became known as "the Hero of Niagara." Over the years, he saved other people from ice floes and kept boats from going over the Falls. He died in 1942, only 54 years old.

Hill's sons carried on the family tradition. So famous and daring were the Hill family rescuers that a movie, *The Great Niagara*, was made about them.

One son, named Major Lloyd Hill, almost went over the Falls in a barrel in 1950, but the local police stopped him. Red Hill Jr., however, was not as lucky. In 1951 he went over the Falls in a flimsy contraption and died.

Wesley Hill, another son of Red, is called "the Watchdog of the Niagara." Like his father, he has recovered hundreds of bodies from the gorge, and he has worked with the police to rescue stranded people and boats. The Hill family is a living part of Niagara Falls history.

CHAPTER 7

Falling Water

THE falls at Niagara are about 12,000 years old. That may seem old to you, but it's young compared with some waterfalls in the world. In Africa and South America, for example, some falls are up to 2.5 million years old. By that standard, the waterfalls at Niagara are still babies!

How were the Falls formed? During the Glacial (Pleistocene) Epoch of the Earth's history (500,000 to 2 million years ago), glaciers melted and formed lakes. Lake Algonquin (located about where Lake Erie is now) overflowed and ran downhill toward Lake Iroquois (about where Lake Ontario is now). The rushing waters, what we know as the Niagara River, chewed out a channel on the path to Lake Iroquois. Today this is called the Niagara Gorge. The Falls were made when the riverbed dropped off suddenly and steeply, like an underwater cliff. Water rushed over this cliff, forming one of the world's most spectacular waterfalls.

NIAGARA FALLS BY BOAT

Let's explore the Niagara River by taking an imaginary boat trip. You hop into a boat on Lake Erie and before long you have entered the Niagara River. The river flows 35 miles (56.3 kilometers) to Lake Ontario. About 14 miles (22.5 kilometers) from the Falls the river splits and travels in two channels around Grand Island, New York. Until it reaches the upper rapids, the river is about 20 feet (6 meters) deep and travels at about 5 miles (8 kilometers) per hour. As you pass Grand Island and later Navy Island, you might recall the stories about William Lyon Mackenzie and his rebels. Imagine the chaos of that night when he fled after his rebellion failed. But keep well aware of where your boat is heading. The rapids you are approaching are only 3 miles (4.8 kilometers) away from the Falls. You'd better paddle for shore now, because the waters hurtle at speeds up to 42 miles

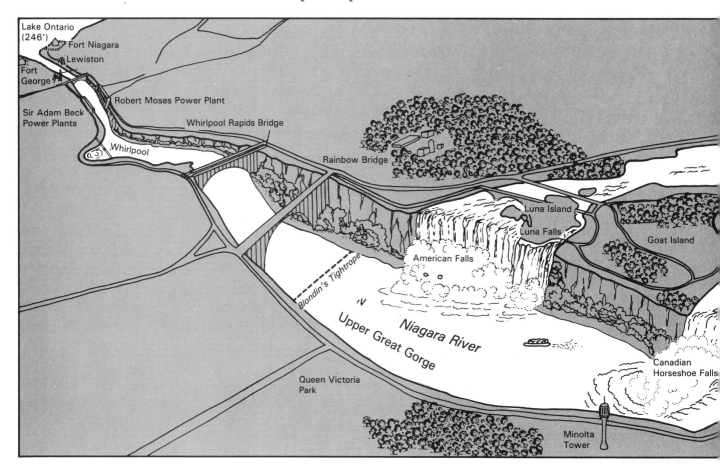

(68 kilometers) per hour to the crest of the Falls and over. Watch out!

The falls at Niagara are actually two waterfalls in one. The American Falls are separated from the Canadian (or Horseshoe) Falls by Goat Island. The American Falls themselves are split into a major waterfall, or cataract, and a beautiful smaller fall, or cascade, called Luna Falls. This cascade is sometimes called Bridal Veil Falls. Between these two American waterfalls is tiny Luna Island. The largest waterfall is the Horseshoe or Canadian Falls, named by the early explorers.

After rushing over the edge of the Falls, the river's waters flow to the Whirlpool Rapids, a pool of turbulent waters 125 feet (38 meters) deep. The Niagara River then winds through the Niagara Gorge, past historic Queenston Heights and Fort George, past Lewiston and Fort Niagara, into Lake Ontario.

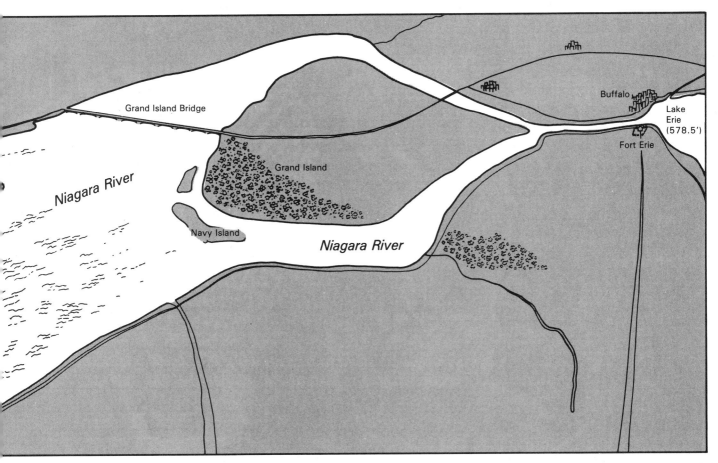

NIAGARA FALLS ON THE MOVE

If you could step into a time-travel machine and press the button for 10,000 B.C., not long after the Falls were formed, you would be in for a surprise. The Falls wouldn't look as they do on postcards today. For one thing, they would be at Queenston-Lewiston, about 7 miles (11 kilometers) from their present location! Through the centuries the rushing waters have worn away the rock under the waterfalls. The point where the water actually drops off the cliff keeps moving back, or receding, toward Lake Erie. This wearing away of the underlying rock is called erosion.

Waterfalls are eroded at different rates. How fast they are eaten up depends on the height of the falls, the amount of water flowing over them and the type of rock under the falls. You can see in the map how the falls at Niagara have "moved" up the river as they have been eroded. Scientists think that the Falls may one day recede all the way back to Lake Erie. However, this won't happen for thousands of years.

Other Waterfalls in North America

The falls at Niagara are only 190 feet (58 meters) high. They are dwarfed by some other waterfalls in North America. Here are the top 10 falls in North America:

1. Yosemite Falls, California
   2,425 feet (739 meters)
2. Ribbon Falls, California
   1,612 feet (491 meters)
3. Upper Yosemite Falls, California
   1,430 feet (436 meters)
4. Takakkaw Falls, British Columbia
   1,300 feet (380 meters)
5. Twin Falls, British Columbia
   975 feet (275 meters)
6. Hunlen Falls, British Columbia
   820 feet (250 meters)
7. Multnomah Falls, Oregon
   680 feet (207 meters)
8. Panther Falls, Alberta
   600 feet (185 meters)
9. Feather Falls, California
   640 feet (195 meters)
10. Bridalveil Falls, California
    620 feet (189 meters)

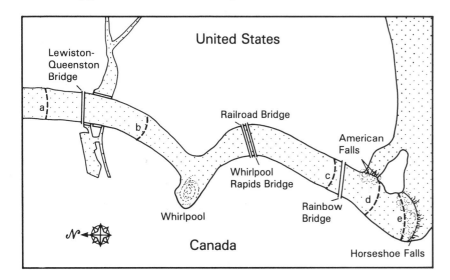

The position of the Falls

a. 12,000 years ago
b. 8,000 years ago
c. 2,000 years ago
d. 700 years ago
e. 300 years ago

The United States and Canadian governments are trying to slow down the erosion of the Falls. The Horseshoe Falls in particular have lost great chunks of rock each year. Some of the rushing water has been channelled around the Falls to hydroelectric power plants, and iron rods have been used to strengthen the rock underneath. These remedies have helped keep the Falls from falling. Today the Horseshoe Falls lose only about 1 foot (30 centimeters) of rock a year, and the American Falls barely erode at all.

When you stand on the shore looking at the waterfalls at Niagara, the clouds of mist sometimes make it difficult to pick out their shapes. Most waterfalls have a smooth, rounded crestline, or edge; sometimes the crestline looks like an arch broken by a V-shaped notch. The notch shows where the crestline is weakest; the edge has broken because the greatest flow of water thunders over that point. Over the years, the crestline changes, following this pattern:

⬚ Hard cap rock

⬚ Softer rock

1. The mass of the rushing waters causes the soft shale and sandstone to weaken underneath the stronger dolomite cap rock.
2. A piece of dolomite breaks off, forming a notch, and the waterfall recedes.
3. The powerful waters smooth out the notch by slow erosion. The crestline is smooth again, un-notched.

This cycle repeats itself over and over again at Niagara.

Waterfalls

Waterfalls occur when water flows over a cliff. The cliffs can be formed in different ways:

- Glaciers may have moved across the land, making grooves in the surface.
- The Earth's surface may have shifted and broken because of pressures building up underground.
- Land may have been eroded, or eaten away, by water.
- Volcanic lava and ice jams may have made barriers in rivers, causing them to change direction and make new channels in the landscape.

The Big Splash

When you visit Niagara Falls, you will probably be impressed by their height. But about 50 other waterfalls in the world are "taller" than Niagara. The Angel Falls (Churun Meru) on the Churun River in Venezuela are first in height. They are 3,212 feet (979 meters) high, compared with the American Falls' 190 feet (58 meters). (The Canadian Horseshoe Falls are 6 feet [2 meters] shorter.) However, some of the tallest falls in the world have very little water flowing over them; they look like trickles of water on the side of a cliff.

It's the combination of height and water flow, or volume, that makes Niagara Falls so beautiful. More than 6 million cubic feet (168,000 cubic meters) of water go over the crestline every minute during the peak daytime tourist hours. That's about a million bathtubsful of water going over the Falls *every second*!

Unraveling the Mysteries of the Falls

Waterfalls leave clues about their history. One of the first places scientists look for clues is the plunge pool (also called a plunge basin) in the riverbed directly beneath the falling waters.

The depth of a plunge pool varies with each waterfall. In some cases, the plunge pool is as deep as the waterfall is tall. For example, the Horseshoe Falls are 185 feet (57 meters) high and their plunge pool is 180 feet (56 meters) deep — almost the same.

Geologists (scientists who study the origin, history and structure of the Earth) can find out about the history of the Falls by measuring the plunge pool depths along the river floor. The longer the Falls stay at a particular point, the deeper the plunge pool at that point will be. The Niagara River has a number of old plunge pools. Scientists can measure the pools and tell how long the Falls were located at any one place.

Ninety per cent of the water at Niagara Falls thunders over the crestline of the Horseshoe Falls. Into that plunge pool are carried the bits of rock that break off the crestline. The American Falls, which get only 10 per cent of the water, barely have a plunge pool. Because there isn't room under the water for all the rock that breaks off at the American Falls, some boulders remain in sight. This debris is called talus.

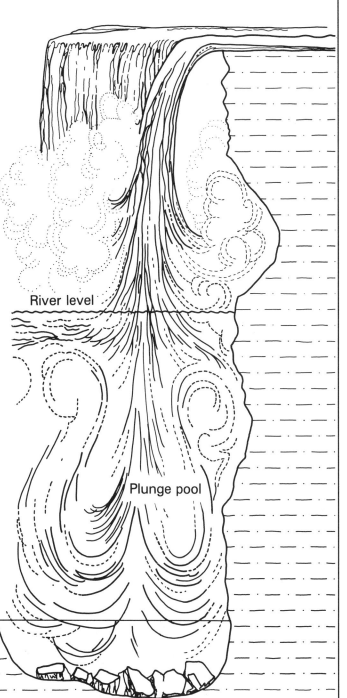

River level

Plunge pool

River bottom

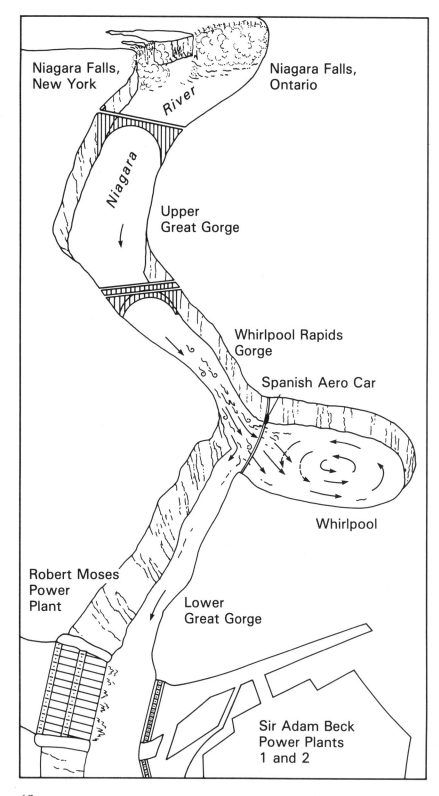

Niagara Falls, New York

Niagara Falls, Ontario

Niagara River

Upper Great Gorge

Whirlpool Rapids Gorge

Spanish Aero Car

Whirlpool

Robert Moses Power Plant

Lower Great Gorge

Sir Adam Beck Power Plants 1 and 2

The Whirlpool

Some Niagara daredevils have lost their lives in the Whirlpool Rapids near the base of the Falls or in the Whirlpool itself. The rapids are formed as the thundering water that has gone over the Falls jounces and blasts over the rocky riverbed below.

In the Whirlpool you can see the "reversal phenomenon." The waters travel over the rapids and enter the pool but then travel counterclockwise around the pool, past the natural outlet. Pressure builds up when the water tries to cut across itself to reach the outlet, and this pressure forces the water *under* the incoming stream. The swirling waters create a vortex, or whirlpool. Then the waters continue their journey to Lake Ontario.

If the water level is low, because water is being diverted for hydro-electric purposes, the reversal does not take place; the waters merely move through the pool and pass to the outlet.

Since 1916 tourists have been able to cross the Whirlpool by travelling on the Spanish Aero Car, designed and built by Spanish engineers. The cable car travels 1,800 feet (549 meters) across the river, giving you a great perspective for photographs of the seething waters.

The Welland Canal

In 1818, a merchant in nearby St. Catharines, Ontario, named William Hamilton Merritt suggested building a canal that would go *around* Niagara Falls. He wanted ships to be able to travel from Lake Ontario to Lake Erie, a trip that was impossible at the time because the Falls were in the way. Merritt's Welland Canal, running from Port Dalhousie on Lake Ontario to the Welland River, was completed in 1829. In 1833 the canal was extended all the way to Port Colborne on Lake Erie.

The Welland Canal has expanded since its early days and is now 27 miles (43.5 kilometers) long. It has a series of locks, which are like elevators for ships. When a ship goes into a lock, the water level in the lock can be raised or lowered, and the ship is raised or lowered with it.

Climbing and descending are part of life for the many ships travelling up and down the Great Lakes waterway. Lake Erie is 325 feet (100 meters) higher than Lake Ontario, and without Merritt's canal ships would still be unable to travel between the two.

Welland Canal profile

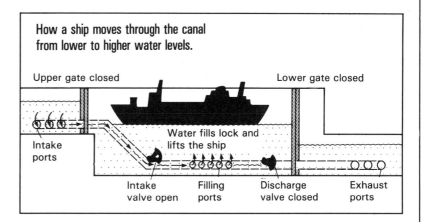

How a ship moves through the canal from lower to higher water levels.

Upper gate closed — Lower gate closed

Intake ports

Water fills lock and lifts the ship

Intake valve open — Filling ports — Discharge valve closed — Exhaust ports

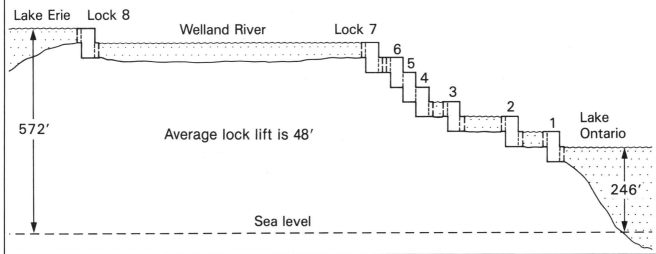

Lake Erie — Lock 8 — Welland River — Lock 7 — 6 5 4 3 2 1 — Lake Ontario

572'

Average lock lift is 48'

246'

Sea level

CHAPTER 8

The Power of Niagara

Sir Adam Beck

Robert Moses

IT'S hard to imagine going anywhere without electricity today. We take it for granted: we flick a switch or push a button and we have light, heat, air conditioning and entertainment. And we can shut it off just as easily. Unlike some other energy forms, electricity cannot be stored, so it is produced around the clock and carefully monitored.

The waters that hypnotize you at Niagara Falls are the same waters that produce millions of kilowatts of electricity. Energy from the rushing water is transformed into electrical energy in huge power plants downstream from the Falls. Because this energy is produced by water, it is called hydro-electricity. The Canadian power plants produce enough power at Niagara Falls to light up almost 20 million 100-watt bulbs at once. Or to supply almost all of the electricity demands of Toronto and Hamilton for a whole year.

That's what millions of kilowatts of hydro-electricity can do. Just *one* kilowatt can

- light ten 100-watt bulbs
- operate one electric iron or two washing machines
- operate three color television sets
- operate one hair dryer or 67 electric razors

THE HISTORY OF NIAGARA POWER

Early settlers near the Falls quickly found that the power of the rushing river could be harnessed and put to use by channelling the water so that it flowed over huge paddlewheels. The water turned the paddlewheels, which turned huge grindstones that ground grain. Canals were built to carry water from the river to mills on the American side of the river. Later, water-powered mills were replaced with factories run by hydro-electricity. Although these factories did not add to the beauty of the area, they did employ lots of people and therefore helped the area grow.

Today there are huge power plants on either side of the river. Two power plants on the Canadian side were the brain children of Adam Beck. He was the first chairman of Ontario Hydro and wanted cheap electrical power to be available to everyone. Sir Adam Beck - Niagara Generating Station No. 1 (built in 1922) and No. 2 (built in 1954) were named after him.

On the American side, a man named Robert Moses spearheaded the building of the power plant which is named after him. Construction of the plant started in 1958. It was completed in 1963. Today it produces 13 billion kilowatt-hours of electricity a year. The amount of concrete used to build the Robert Moses plant would be enough to pave a two-lane highway 973 miles (1,556 kilometers) long. That's one-third of the distance across North America. No wonder Robert Moses is sometimes called "New York's Master Builder."

Now *That's* Big!
Niagara Falls produces energy for millions of North Americans. The machines built to generate the power are as big as the job itself:

- The rotor of the generator weighs as much as 119 elephants, the shaft weighs as much as 11 elephants, and the turbine weighs as much as 15 elephants.
- The Robert Moses Power Plant in New York has a reservoir that holds enough water to fill 20 Olympic swimming pools.

INSIDE A HYDRO-ELECTRIC PLANT

"Hydro-electricity" is made by converting the natural power of running water into energy we can use. Today hydro-electricity lights homes and factories in many parts of the world. Best of all, hydro-electricity is a renewable and non-polluting source of energy. And it's fast — it takes only 30 minutes for a bucket of water to travel through the entire system and produce electricity! Here's what happens:

— Water above the Falls pours into gathering tubes 500 feet (152 meters) long, which are submerged at the shoreline.

— From the tubes, the water flows into two concrete-lined tunnels. These tunnels, located below ground, are just over 46 feet (14 meters) in diameter. Gates can close off the tunnels to stop the flow if there are any problems at the power stations.

— The water collects in a reservoir called a forebay. Every minute, 29 million gallons (109 million liters) of water travel through the tunnels into the forebay serving the two Adam Beck stations. No pumping is needed to get the water from the forebay to the generating units. The forebay is on higher ground than the river, so gravity pulls the water into motion.

— There are 16 generating units at the Beck Station No. 2. Together they can produce nearly 2 million horsepower. (Your family car runs on about 100 horsepower.)

— The water rushes down a pipe, called a penstock, into the turbines. The turbines power the generators, and soon electricity will be on its way into homes and businesses. (To see how a generator works, see the box on this page.)

— The water exits through another pipe, called the tailrace, into the river below the Falls.

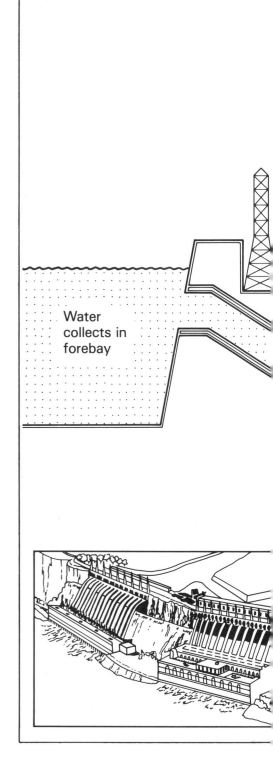

Water collects in forebay

The power station tunnels are big enough to drive a car through.

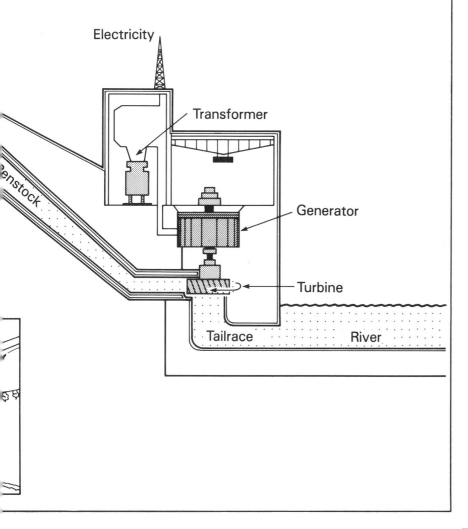

Electricity

Transformer

Generator

Turbine

Penstock

Tailrace

River

How a generator works

A generating unit at a hydro-electric plant is made up of two parts — the turbine and the generator. Together they convert the energy of flowing water into electrical energy.

The turbine has a paddle-wheel called a turbine runner, which works like a windmill. Running water spins the wheel, which turns the turbine shaft.

The shaft then turns the generator shaft and spins magnets inside a coil of wire. The wires conduct electricity to the outside of the generator through a grid of transformers and power lines to where it is needed.

HOW ELECTRICITY GETS TO YOU

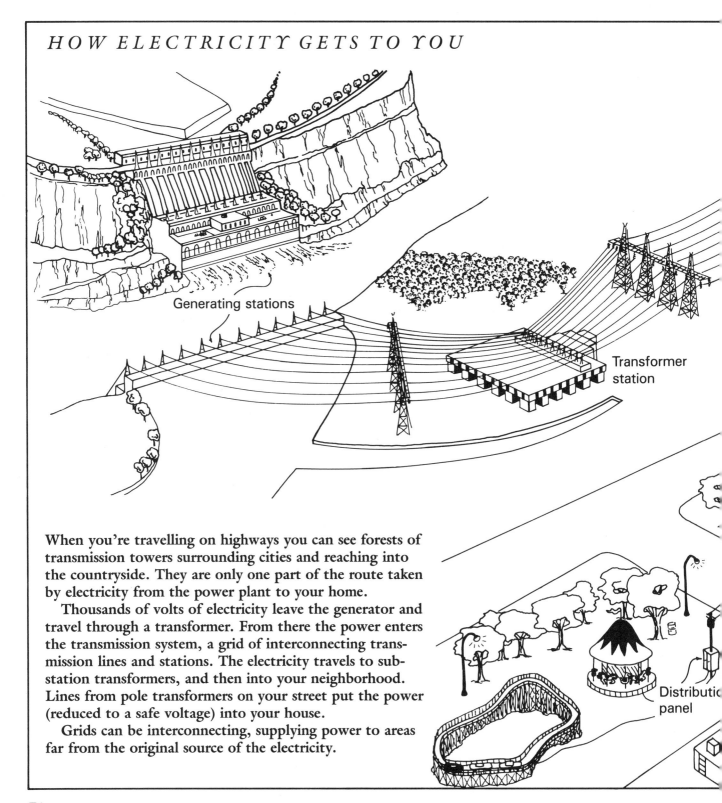

Generating stations

Transformer station

Distribution panel

When you're travelling on highways you can see forests of transmission towers surrounding cities and reaching into the countryside. They are only one part of the route taken by electricity from the power plant to your home.

Thousands of volts of electricity leave the generator and travel through a transformer. From there the power enters the transmission system, a grid of interconnecting transmission lines and stations. The electricity travels to substation transformers, and then into your neighborhood. Lines from pole transformers on your street put the power (reduced to a safe voltage) into your house.

Grids can be interconnecting, supplying power to areas far from the original source of the electricity.

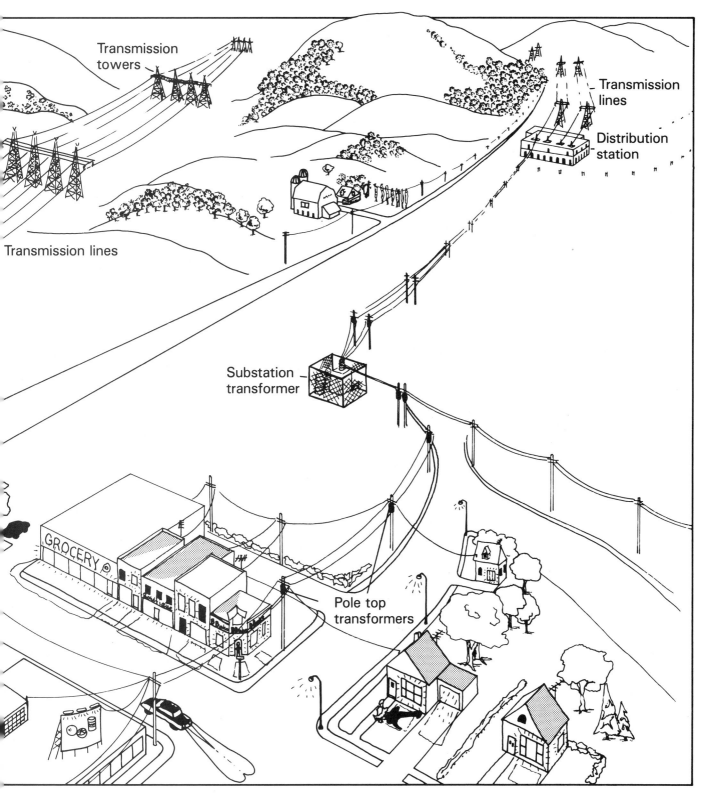

Transmission towers

Transmission lines

Transmission lines

Distribution station

Substation transformer

GROCERY

Pole top transformers

TURNING OFF THE FALLS?

If you visit the Falls after dark in the summer, you will see only about half the amount of water going over the crest that a daytime tourist would see. It's hard to tell the difference, but it's there. The water is being channelled away, or "diverted," from the Falls by the power plants. To make sure Niagara Falls never runs dry, the power plants signed a special treaty, called the Niagara Diversion Treaty, in 1950.

During the daylight hours in the peak tourist season at least 100,000 cubic feet (3,000 cubic meters) per second must flow over the crestline of the two waterfalls. At night and during the rest of the year, the flow is cut in half. The rest of the water is divided equally between the United States and Canada for generating hydro-electricity. Thanks to this arrangement, Niagara Falls' rushing waters will continue to amaze and astound tourists, stunters, sketchers and honeymooners as they have for hundreds of years.

Pollution and the Niagara River

We hear more each year about the pollution of the Niagara River. One well-known case is the Love Canal.

Love Canal is located at the south end of Niagara Falls, New York. The name comes from William Love, a real estate promoter in the area in the 1890s. Until the 1950s, the area was used as a dumping site for chemical waste from manufacturing plants in the region. A neighborhood with homes and a school was built on the property later.

In 1978, the name Love Canal came into the news when the long-buried chemicals worked their way to the surface. They caused burns on the feet of children and pets. Eighty-two different chemicals were found in the water and soil. People began to worry that the chemicals could cause cancer and birth abnormalities.

Officials have discovered that the chemicals from Love Canal and more than 200 other dumpsites are still seeping into the Niagara River. The governments of the United States and Canada are studying how to clean up the river and prevent future pollution.

Illustrations

Sandi Hemsworth: maps on pages 8, 38, 62-63, 64, 68; diagrams on pages 65, 67, 69, 72-73, 74-75
Pat Cupples: all other illustrations

Photographs

Every effort has been made to locate the copyright holders for the photographs included in the book. If anyone has been unintentionally omitted, the publishers would be pleased to receive notification for future printings.

p. 8 Archives of Ontario; p. 9 (left) New York Power Authority (right) Cal Smiley; p. 10 Archives of Ontario; p. 11 (left) The Niagara Parks Commission (right) Cal Smiley; p. 12 The Niagara Parks Commission; p. 13 (right) Cal Smiley (left) The Niagara Parks Commission; p. 14 The Niagara Parks Commission; p. 19 Royal Ontario Museum, Toronto; p. 24 Archives of Ontario; p. 28 Ontario Hydro; p. 31, 34 Archives of Ontario; p. 43 The Niagara Parks Commission; p. 45 Ontario Hydro; p. 48 Archives of Ontario; p. 49, 57, 58 The Niagara Parks Commission; p. 70 (top) Ontario Hydro (bottom) New York Power Authority; p. 71 New York Power Authority; p. 73 Ontario Hydro. All other photographs, the author.

Text

P. 49: from the Journals of Mary O'Brien, 1828-1838, edited by Audrey Saunders Miller, 1968. Reprinted by permission of Macmillan of Canada

Index